Anne-Katrin Hagen

First
Steps in Dressage

Basic training for horse and rider

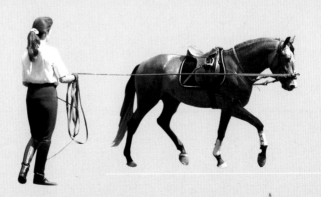

CADMOS
EQUESTRIAN

Contents

Introduction

Although the term used is "dressage", it would be more correct to refer to "gymnastic exercises". It is impossible to teach a horse something that it cannot do by natural design! The difficulty lies in drawing out the natural capability of the horse and then shaping it into something beautiful and expressive. The horse must learn how to balance under the rider and move in elegant self-carriage with more weight on the hindquarters. The horse's hindquarters must be developed to carry more weight and improve forward propulsion. The horse's centre of gravity lies considerably far to the front, just behind the shoulder blade, due to the neck and heavy head. Gymnastic exercises transfer this point further back.

The goal of training a horse is that it moves gracefully in all the gaits and reacts to feather-light aids.

To reach this goal, the rider needs a lot of experience. Thus the golden rule: a young inexperienced horse needs an experienced rider, and an inexperienced rider needs an experienced horse. The most important prerequisite is that the rider must be capable of giving the aids. The rider must have a correct, independent seat and be able to give clear and precise aids: the hands quiet and leg and back aids deliberate and exact. This must be maintained in the dressage seat as well as the forward seat and in all aspects of riding. Jumps of joy and bucks from the horse should not be allowed to disconcert the rider.

The goal is to bring the natural centre of gravity (top) more under the horse (bottom) with the correct gymnastic exercises.

The ideal dressage seat should be without any tension.
Photo: P. Prohn

The Correct Seat

Without a good seat, the training of a young horse is impossible. The first exercises and lessons demand an independent seat and correct, finely tuned aids. A correct seat is the basis for good riding in all disciplines.

In the dressage seat one sits in the middle of the saddle, well balanced both laterally and vertically, with the legs hanging long and loose at the sides of the horse, the balls of the feet resting lightly in the stirrups. The heels are the lowest point of the rider, the feet parallel to the horse so the calf lies flat on the body of the horse. Only thus can the ankles spring up and down with the movement.

The upper body is upright, the head carried free and the eyes look forward through the horse's ears. The shoulders are taken back a fraction and relaxed, the arms hang down quite naturally. Close the fist (the thumbs on top like a roof) and bend the elbows so that the fists are approximately a hand's width from the withers. There should be an imaginary vertical line through the ear, shoulder, hip and ankle when the rider sits in this natural and completely relaxed manner. The lower arm and the reins will naturally form a straight line to the horse's mouth and the lower leg will rest just behind the girth. Seen from behind, the rider's spine forms a vertical line with the horse's croup and tail, and the rider's shoulders, hips and feet form parallel lines to the ground.

Only from such a balanced and relaxed seat can precise aids be given. Relaxation must not

The rider's shoulders, hips and heels should be parallel to the ground; the rider's spine should form a vertical line with the horse's croup and tail. Photo: P. Prohn

• leg aids, forward driving, forward sideways or supporting
• rein aids, active, yielding, blocking, supporting and directional.

Finely tuned aids, presented from a correct seat, are the only way to achieve harmonious collaboration between horse and rider in all the gaits. Fundamentally, the driving aids (body and legs) are more important than the supporting aids (reins).

Body aids

When equal weight is disposed on both sides of the saddle, the seat bones are matched in their weight-load. The upper body stays upright and the abdominal muscles are tightened. This is called "bracing the back". A good analogy is to imagine riding on a big tube of toothpaste: by tipping the hips both legs can be applied energetically while the hands can give, to "let the toothpaste out" at the front. This is not a permanent aid but lasts only a moment. "Bracing the back" is a sign for the hindquarters to become more active. Depending on how energetic the aids are, the horse will walk from halt, or even trot on.

be compromised when the rider tries to stay in this accurate position. Shoulders, elbows, wrists, hips, knees and ankles must remain free, not full of tension. A horse cannot move freely under a rigid rider!

The aids are the means by which the rider communicates with the horse; and they are:

• body aids, equal weight on both sides, unilateral weight

"Bracing the back"

A collapsed hip puts the rider's weight on the wrong side. Photo: P. Prohn

A slightly inclined upper body takes the weight off the horse's back.
Photo: P. Prohn

The unilateral weight aid is used when the horse is flexed in one direction, for transitions and for assisting directional rein aids. When, for example, the horse must turn to the right, the right seat bone of the rider goes forward and down while the hips remain braced. The pelvis should remain stretched when giving leg aids as well.

A lighter seat is used when the horse's back and hindquarters need to move more freely. The backside remains in the saddle but the weight goes more onto the upper leg and knee, while the upper body leans slightly forward. This aid is useful when training young horses, riding up gentle slopes and the first attempt at reining back.

Leg aids

The forward driving leg aids drive the horse forward in all paces with the rider's leg just behind the girth applying light pressure.

The forward-sideways leg aids are used in lateral work like leg-yielding where the leg of the rider lies a hand's width behind the girth; the knee and ankle must not be pulled up. The forward-sideways driving leg aid is supported by the movement of the rider's weight.

The supporting leg aid is used opposite the forward-sideways driving aid where it stops the hindquarters from falling out. The supporting leg is also placed about one hand's breadth from the girth, but is not as active.

Against the hand; the horse tries to pull the reins out of the rider's hands.

Rein aids

The rein aids are never used alone. Only a horse that is "through" allows the rein aids to work from the mouth over the poll, the neck and back into the hindquarters. The horse lets the aids through, making it "permeable".

With the active rein aid the fist is closed or slightly turned to the inside for a moment in order to shorten the rein a little. Pulling on the reins is frowned upon.

The active aid is always followed by the yielding rein aid. The fists return to their normal position with the fingers relaxed. This does not mean the contact to the horse's mouth must be broken; it should always be there, even with the yielding rein aid.

Blocking rein aids are used when the horse goes against the hand or above the reins. The

Above the reins; the horse does not give in the poll, opens its mouth and hollows its back.

The horse stretches forwards and downwards. The contact to the rider's hand stays intact. Photo: W. Ernst

fists are in position, the back is braced and the legs are driving forward energetically. The heaviness that arises from this must be endured until the horse gives in and becomes light in the hand. This moment must not be missed, for the hands must immediately become relaxed and the seat soft. This way the horse will know what we want from him.

Directional rein aids are used when a horse must move on a curve, for example on a leftward circle. The left rein is turned in very slightly and the horse's left eye and nostril become just visible. The right hand yields. The directional rein aid is always given with the supporting aid that helps to maintain the curve. The supporting rein is the counterpart of the directional rein aid. These aids are always given with the unilateral driving leg aid and the one-sided weight aid.

Directional rein aids help the young horse in its orientation of the bend. This rein also assists in teaching horses lateral movements.

There is no contact on the rein. The horse moves freely with its nose in a low position. Photo: P. Prohn

Accompanied by the relevant body aid, the hand is taken away slightly into the direction in which the horse must move. Once the horse accepts this aid, the hand must yield to follow the active hand.

Rein aids are not to be given alone! The reins alone cannot force the horse to give in the poll.

A horse that has even and continuous contact on both reins and is foaming while chewing is considered to be "on the bit". "On a long rein" means the rider still has contact with the horse's mouth, but the horse moves in a natural way with its nose lower and its neck longer. "On a free rein" means the rider has only the buckle of the rein in the hand and the horse is moving with a free head and neck carriage and no contact to the rider's hand.

Knees, legs and weight in the stirrups take over from the seat bones. The reins are shortened. Photo: P. Prohn

The forward seat

There are many disciplines in riding where the forward seat is used, but it is mainly to take the rider's weight off the horse's back and is mostly ridden in a jumping or eventing saddle. The style of these saddles (forward cut flap and knee rolls, longer and flatter seat) makes it easier to ride in the forward seat. The stirrups are shortened considerably: Two holes when riding young horses or going for a hack, and four to five holes when jumping or eventing. Naturally the rider's height and the length of leg also require adjustment of the stirrup length. In the forward seat the rider can more easily adapt to the movement of the horse,

changing position with the centre of gravity. When jumping, or riding up or downhill, the rider can move the upper body, depending on how much weight should be taken off the horse's back. The foundation of knee, lower leg, ankle and foot in the stirrup stays in place.

What does the forward seat look like? Depending on the amount of weight taken off the horse's back, the upper body inclines from the hips. The seat leaves the saddle more in a higher tempo, for example the gallop or jumping, but the rider's posture stays elastic and in the correct position. The same principle applies for both the dressage seat and the forward seat; a stiff, fidgety upper body with tight, hunched shoulders and a hollow back is not only wrong, but will also disturb the horse.

The knee lies tighter on the saddle, and the angle at the knee is more pronounced. Losing the close contact of the knee with the saddle leaves the rider vulnerable. The lower leg lies on the girth and takes over the driving action. Should the lower leg slip to the rear or start to swing to and fro the rider will lose balance. The heel is the lowest point of the rider, and the ankle remains soft to absorb the movement. The shoulder, knee and stirrup are in a line in the forward seat, the head in front of the parallel and the hips to the back where they build up momentum to help with the driving force of the leg. If the heel gets pulled up and the lower leg retreats to the

The horse makes a bigger movement over the fence, the rider's body must also make a bigger movement
Photo: P. Prohn

back, the rider will fall in front of the movement. The head is carried naturally free and the eyes look between the ears of the horse, as in the dressage seat. The shoulders are relaxed and the arms are moved to the front of the body, with the reins taken shorter in order to maintain a straight line from elbow to horse's mouth. The hands are held at the side of the neck, more or less in front of the withers. In the forward seat the aids from the hands and legs are used independently from the movement of the upper body.

The aids are, in principle, the same in the dressage seat and the forward seat. With the weight taken off the seat, the body aids are given more from the knee and stirrup. The important thing to remember with the rein aids is that the outside rein is predominant, especially in turns at the canter.

When riding young horses it is often necessary to use the sideways rein aids together with more weight on the inside stirrup. Young horses are almost "driven" in the forward seat, rather than ridden.

The lunge line should not be slack. The young horse may not run out of the circle. Pressure on the lunge should be even and gentle. Photo: C. Slawik

Prerequisites for the Horse

The horse must be taught on the lunge to move in a relaxed and rhythmical way in all three gaits without leaving the circle, letting the outside hind fall out or any other deviation from the circle.

This way the rider can concentrate on the way the horse moves: Does he have difficulty maintaining balance? Does he find it hard to follow into the footprints of the front feet? Does he find it easy to stretch forwards and down? How active is his walk after a demanding canter?

All these points can determine how the horse should be trained.

The Basic Gaits

There are three basic gaits: walk, trot and canter. Each gait has a different pace or tempo.

Apart from the working pace – the pace at which a young horse finds it easiest to stay balanced – there are the collected, medium and extended paces. In the walk there are simply collected, medium and extended steps.

The walk has four beats or steps. The horse uses his feet one after the other: left hind, left fore, right hind, right fore. There is no moment of suspension. That makes the walk a gait without cadence. It should be diligent and forward-going but not hurried. The horse must move straight forward in a relaxed manner, with even contact on the reins. The four beats can be counted clearly: 1-2-3-4, and so on. When the well-defined four beats are lost (1-2, 3-4) the walk becomes defective. When only two beats are heard, the horse paces and this is a major fault. The medium pace is the only one used with the young horse; the collected walk where the hindquarters step more under the body of the horse, as well as the extended walk where the steps are longer, are only required in higher dressage classes. In order to hold the walk at the correct beat, it is important for the back and poll to stay relaxed. The horse is allowed to stretch slightly for-

The walk is a gait in four beats without cadence.

"One!"   "Two!"

"Three!"   "Four!"

wards and downwards and the hand of the rider softly follows the natural movement of the horse's head. The surest way to do this is by riding on a circle. Never ride in walk for too long! Trot or canter for a while, then come back to a few steps of walking. The walk is the only gait that can be ruined by doing too much of it! On a long rein, however, rider and horse can always recuperate from strenuous exercise.

The trot has two beats. The horse uses diagonal pairs of legs alternately (right hind/left fore and left hind/right fore) In between, there is a moment of suspension, which makes it full of cadence and one can distinguish between collected, working, medium and extended trot. In the first dressage steps the working trot is used and also "lengthening of the steps", which progresses to medium trot. The working trot must be ridden in an active way with the horse swinging rhythmically on a soft contact. The tempo must be such that the horse does not lose rhythm in turns or changes of the hand. To protect the young horse's back, and for comfort, it is advisable to rise to the trot. When the sitting trot is introduced, the knees of the rider must be tight-

The trot is full of cadence in two beats.

"One!"   *"Two!"*

Medium trot: The momentum comes from the hindquarters. The horse takes bigger, flat steps. The rhythm must not be allowed to become faster. Photo: C. Slawik

ened to act as suspension. A few strides are taken before sitting completely and care must be taken that the horse accepts the weight of the rider without changing the rhythm of the trot. It is important that the horse and rider both stay relaxed and the horse moves forward freely. Once that is established a few length-ened strides can be attempted: carefully ride into the corner, make sure the horse is straight on the long side, put both legs tighter on the girth, move the hand slightly to the front and let the horse move forwards energetically with longer strides. No running is allowed (that is apparent when the rhythm gets faster)! Do not lose patience! Lengthening the stride is difficult, even for those horses that have a nat-

Collected trot: The steps become higher, the horse covers less distance. The bounce is maintained but directed upwards. Photo: C. Slawik

"One!"

"Two!"　"Three!"

The canter is a springy gait with a triple beat.

urally good gait. Young horses must learn to balance under the rider's weight and the young rider must adapt to all that movement. The movement of the back in medium trot is a vigorous forward-moving wave that has to be supported by the rider. Unless the rider can maintain an even balance, it is better to do a rising trot.

The canter has three beats and is counted in jumps. There is a differentiation between left and right canter. Normally the left canter is ridden on the left rein, and the right canter on the right rein. In the right canter the horse starts with the left hind, followed by the diagonal right hind and left fore and then the right fore. Next is a moment of suspension that

makes it a gait full of cadence. To make a quick check for the correct lead, the rider can look at the shoulder to see if it travels further to the front. One can definitely count with the canter: 1-2-3, 1-2-3. When counting one, two-and, three, the rhythm is lost. The diagonal feet no longer touch the ground at the same time anymore. To counteract this one must ride forward more energetically. There is collected, working, medium and extended canter, but initially only the working canter is used. Once the young horse understands the aids for canter, he must canter in a clear triple beat with soft contact on the rein in a bouncy manner.

The movement of the canter is such that it is much easier for the rider to remain seated, than

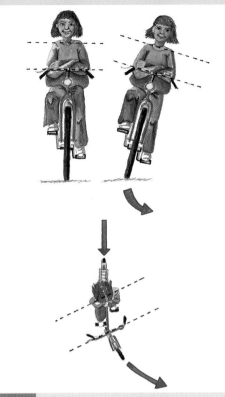

An extremely good exercise for a young horse is to canter in the country, nose lower than in the arena to round the back more, with plenty of drive but in control. This way the young horse can jump more easily with a lower centre of gravity and balance himself rapidly. Cantering in the country should only be attempted once the young horse and the young rider have developed enough confidence in the arena. A runaway horse in the country is too dangerous! These first attempts at cantering in the country should always be in the company of an experienced older horse.

Balance is everything! The same principle applies for riding a bicycle around a corner – without hands – as when riding a horse through a corner.

With rounded back and lowered nose the horse canters with enthusiasm. The rider should, however, wear a hard hat. Photo: C. Slawik

in the trot so there are fewer problems in this area. It is also easier for the young horse to find his balance in the canter. Like riding a bicycle, it is easier to ride fast, but going slow can cause problems! Problems occur in turns and corners. A lot of young horses will change at the back to try and keep their balance: they support themselves with the outside hind. The rider must keep the bend around the corners and on the circle must keep the outside rein in strong contact, helping the horse in this way to put the inside hind more under the body and so to stay in balance.

The nose should be slightly in front of the vertical, the poll the highest point of the horse. Photo: W. Ernst

Rhythm, Suppleness and Contact

Body and leg aids from behind into the hand. Picture a flow of energy that spirals from the rider's head through his back into the pelvis. There it strengthens and glides along the legs to enclose the whole horse from behind in a circle of energy.

The first steps of training a young horse and rider are so intertwined that it is hard to tell them apart. No horse can move under a rider without contact, suppleness or rhythm. The horse must be "on the aids", meaning it must be ridden on the weight and leg aids, from the back into the hand. There can then develop a feather-light contact between the horse and rider. The nose of the horse must be slightly ahead of the vertical and the poll the highest

Tail, ears, lips softened – this is what a relaxed horse should look like. Photo: C. Slawik

Exercises for Relaxation and Gymnastics

Riding on a circle

Riding the young horse on a circle is the next step. The horse will be familiar with the circle from being lunged and will have already learned to keep a slight bend by adapting to the line of the circle from poll to tail. The rider puts more weight on the inside seat bone and the inside leg drives the inside hind of the

The rider's shoulders are parallel to those of the horse. The outside rein releases a little to form a slight bend. However, it remains the leading rein. Photo: P. Prohn

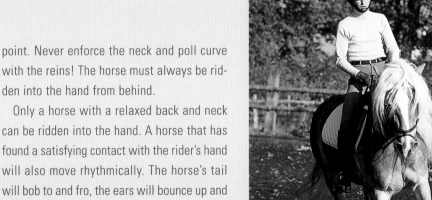

point. Never enforce the neck and poll curve with the reins! The horse must always be ridden into the hand from behind.

Only a horse with a relaxed back and neck can be ridden into the hand. A horse that has found a satisfying contact with the rider's hand will also move rhythmically. The horse's tail will bob to and fro, the ears will bounce up and down and a white frothy lather will form on the lips. When the horse then happily snorts on top of that, any rider can feel that something positive has been accomplished!

horse to step forward. The outside leg supports the hindquarters, preventing them from falling out. The inside rein assists the body weight of the rider to bend the horse in order to position the horse (the inside eye and nostril can just be seen— no more!). The outside rein releases just sufficient to allow the bend. The outside rein must prevent too much bend, for that would lead to falling out over the shoulder. To describe it in a different way: the inside rein suggests bend, the outside rein wants to keep the horse straight, the inside leg wants to push the horse out of the circle and the outside leg wants to prevent the hindquarters from leaving the circle. There is a continuous correlation between the "diagonal" aids.

This principle is significant in all exercises on bends. The horse's hind legs must always follow in the path of the front legs, like a train on tracks.

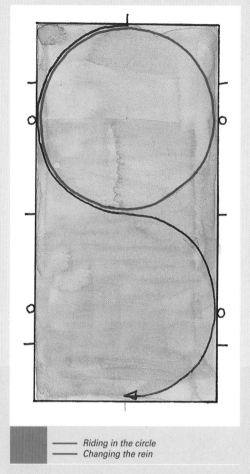

Riding in the circle
Changing the rein

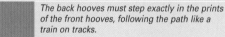
The back hooves must step exactly in the prints of the front hooves, following the path like a train on tracks.

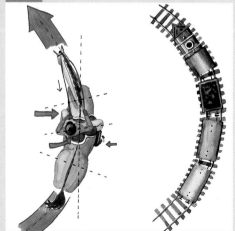

Changing the rein

Once the horse moves in a relaxed, supple and rhythmical way on the favoured rein (most of the time this is the left rein), it is time to change the rein. Ride on straight for approximately two or three horse lengths at the open end of the circle and softly, without being abrupt, change the horse over onto the other rein. When the change is done in rising trot one must change the diagonals as well by sitting twice at X. No change of rhythm or tempo should be allowed and work must continue on the new rein until the horse moves as smoothly on the new rein as on the other rein. Once that has been established the changes can be done more frequently and as soon as the horse is equal on both reins one can start to use the whole arena.

Going large

At the outset it is sensible to return to the circle after riding on the long side of the arena, as that requires much more balance. The horse must move quite straight but with a slight bend to the inside and the inside hind must not be used as a prop anymore. The corners must be ridden in a proper bend right into the circle.

Changing the rein through the diagonal serves as a test for the balance of the young horse as there is no optical boundary to fall back on. Time and patience are required until the horse can move straight and rhythmically in both walk and trot through the diagonal. Once that has been established, the half-halt is brought into the equation more and more.

Half-halt

By now the young horse has learned to accept the forward driving, lateral bending and supporting aids. Now the time is right to put all the aids (body, leg and reins) into the half-halt. The rider puts more weight on the seat, braces the back, drives with the leg and curbs the forward dashing of the horse with blocking rein aids. The rider "compresses" the horse from

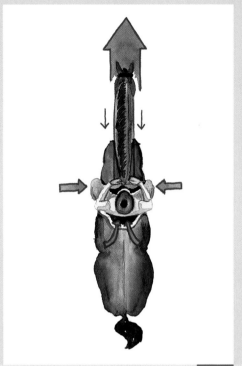

Half–halt: bracing the back, pressure from the legs, blocking the reins, all of these together as a short impulse.

back to front and immediately follows it up with a yielding rein. The half-halt is employed in the form of short impulses from a correct and balanced seat. The half-halt is not a single occurrence but follows the rhythm of the movement. It is used:

- to make transitions from one gait to another
- to regulate the pace in a gait
- to draw the horse's attention to something
- to attain, keep and improve contact and to achieve collection
- to ride the horse altogether properly.

A stronger half–halt results in a halt.

Wrong!

The halt

The halt is asked for only on a straight line and can basically ensue from any gait. A strong half-halt always results in a halt! Increased driving with the weight and legs causes the

horse to step into the blocking hand that yields to become soft just before the horse comes to a standstill. Young horses use their necks as balancing poles to stand quietly with composure. Stepping to and fro, standing with the legs apart and nodding with the head are considered major faults. The last-named indicates an unyielding and unkind hand.

Taking the rein out of the hand

Testing if the horse is "on the aids", supple with a soft contact, is the reason for allowing the horse to take the reins out of the hand. This is possible in every gait, although it is recommended to try it in walk at first, later in the trot and only at the canter when one is completely confident. In the normal working tempo the rider slightly opens the fingers; whereupon the horse searches for the bit by stretching his

Taking the reins out of the hand – when the fingers are opened the horse should look for the bit by stretching forwards and down. Photo: W. Ernst

neck forwards and down, without losing balance and rhythm. The stretch occurs down to the height of the stirrups, with the nose staying in front of the vertical.

The rider's hand follows the horse's mouth without losing contact. It is preferable to execute this exercise often in small stretches, for the danger is that the horse can go onto the forehand if this is done for too long.

On the bit or not?

Acceptance of the bit means that the driving aids and the guiding aids have met. A way to test this is to move the hands up the horse's neck for a duration of approximately two to three horse lengths, and observe if he stays in self-carriage, then return the hands to their normal position. This exercise can be done in all the gaits.

Both hands are moved up the horse's neck for a few seconds. The horse should move on in complete self-carriage.

Transitions

Frequent transitions from one gait to another are excellent gymnastic exercises for the horse and teach the rider use of the correct aids. Once the horse can accomplish smooth and regular transitions from walk to trot and trot to walk, the transition can be attempted at the canter. To start off, it is easier for horse and rider to start against the wall, where the horse will be less tempted to run. To introduce the left rein canter from a sitting trot, the left leg stays on the girth while the right leg moves one hand behind the girth. The right rein actively becomes firm, the left rein yields. The rider transfers weight to the inside, left seat

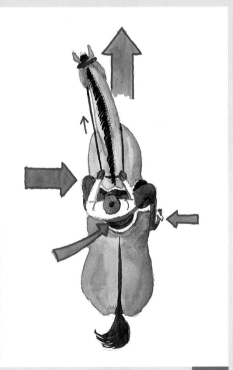

All the aids must be executed at the same time! Pressure from the left leg is stronger. For the right rein canter the aids are mirror image.

A rocking horse – the upper body stays vertical, the angle of the hips and elbows changes.

bone in a forwards and downwards direction and pressure is exerted in this position (remember the tube of toothpaste!). These aids must all be executed at the same time as a big step is taken with the left leg. Do not leave the right shoulder behind! This posture must be maintained during the left canter. Every canter stride must be ridden as if it were the first. The horse moves like a rocking horse in the canter and the rider must balance the strides in the angles of the hips and elbows. The upper body stays relaxed and vertical and the legs lie quietly on the girth, without bobbing to and fro.

When the rider wants to go back into trot, both legs move onto the girth, the rider sits up, takes up active rein contact and sits "into" the horse. The legs drive the horse from the three beats of the canter into the two beats of the trot. This half-halt should move through the whole body of the horse, depositing more weight on the hindquarters. Initially the knee presses firmly in the saddle so as not to fall with all the weight on the horse's back. The change should be clear and precise with no running steps. The same guidelines apply for the trot to walk transition.

The horse steps back with diagonal legs, as in the trot. Photo: P. Prohn

Rein back

When the halt from walk and trot has been successful with the horse in balance and standing on all four feet, the rein back can be implemented. The most important part of the rein back is the effective halt! If the horse is standing with his feet far back, or does not have a soft contact, it is impossible to rein back without resistance. The rein back is stepping back with diagonal legs without dragging the hind feet in the sand. The rider uses the same aids as for riding forwards, but as soon as the horse moves his feet, the rider's weight shifts onto the thigh and knees. The upper

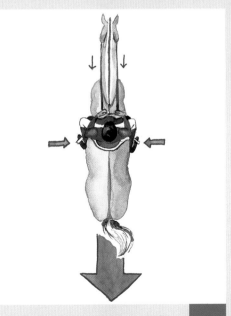

Rein back – in the rein back one must think "forwards".

body should not fall forwards, the legs should support the horse on both sides and the reins should be active. These aids must be administered together, to direct the horse's energy towards the back. After three or four steps, the yielding rein aid follows and the rider sits back into a halt.

Riding turns

The most important concept in riding turns is for the fore and hind legs to follow behind each other, as if in tramlines. This means that the bend must go through the whole body of the horse, not just the neck.

Corners

Just before reaching the end of the arena, the use of one or two half-halts gets the horse's attention and he can be prepared to advance into the corner. The rider's inside seat bone receives more weight and the inside leg has more drive on the girth; the outside leg supports, the outside rein allows the bend to the inside without losing contact.

The change through the diagonal demands a properly ridden corner! The inside leg and outside rein encourage the horse to move through the corner completely before changing. The rider looks at the diagonal point in order to arrive there in a straight line. Once on the track, remember the half-halt for the next corner is due!

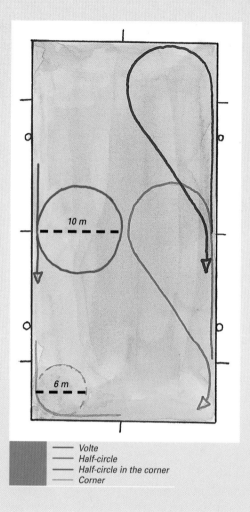

10 m

6 m

——— Volte
——— Half-circle
——— Half-circle in the corner
——— Corner

Volte

At six metres, the volte is the smallest bend possible for a horse; anything smaller cannot be considered a correct bend. This is also the reason why a volte of ten metres in diameter is ridden in the beginning. The volte is round, and ends where it began. The horse must move "in the tracks" with good rhythm and forwards momentum, the aids similar to riding the corner. Sensitivity and patience is needed for an accurate volte; if the inside rein is too tight, the inside leg too strong or the outside leg too weak, the horse will only be pulled around and the hindquarters will fall out.

The first part of the half-circle in the corner is ridden like the volte. At the height of the volte the horse is straightened and ridden back to the track.

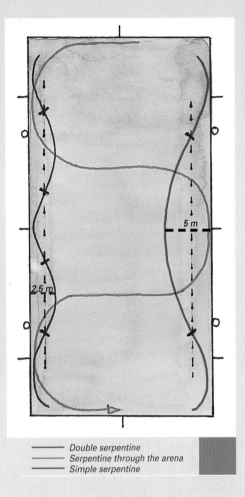

5 m

2.5 m

Double serpentine
Serpentine through the arena
Simple serpentine

Serpentines

The first serpentines are only three or four loops, starting and ending on the short side of the arena. A serpentine of three loops can for example start with one half of a circle at A, rounding it off, straightening the horse for a few strides, changing the bend and riding the next half circle, touching the long side of the arena at HB. Then another straight line and a half circle follow, to bring the horse to C. The purpose of serpentines is to test the willingness of the horse to change the bend and straighten himself.

Serpentines on the long side of the arena are more difficult and are called simple and double serpentines. Simple serpentines are five metres away from the track and double serpentines only two and a half metres away. After correctly riding the corner the horse is bent to the inside and is moved away from the track. Within about two horse lengths the bend is changed so that the outside leg now becomes the inside leg. On the level of HB the horse touches the furthest point, two horse lengths, before the bend is changed again which takes the horse back to the track. In the double serpentine everything happens a bit faster. The furthest the horse moves away from the track is two and a half metres and in between the horse returns to the track at HB. This means the change in bend happens relatively quickly and the rider must be sure of the aids. All stiffness from both horse and rider will be noticed immediately, which makes the double serpentine a worthy test for an independent seat from the rider and suppleness from the horse.

Leg-yielding

Leg-yielding is a suppling exercise and makes the future use of lateral aids easier. The inside leg drives the horse more into the outside hand and the horse moves in a forwards-sideways direction on two tracks without bending. The rider puts more weight on the inside seat bone, with the inside leg driving the horse and the outside leg supporting behind the girth to keep the forward movement. The inside rein is slightly active while the outside rein keeps the shoulder from falling out.

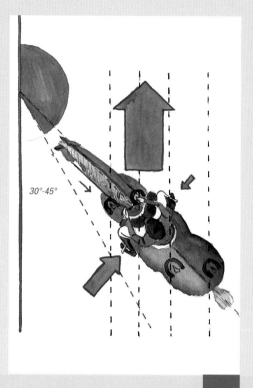

Leg-yielding – the horse must stay straight! The inside leg drives into the outside rein.

Exercises in leg-yielding

This exercise is ridden diagonally to the side of the arena with the horse moving away from the track, making the horse obedient to the forwards-sideways driving leg and the leading, restricting outside rein.

From the corner the rider slightly bends the horse to the outside and pushes with the new inside leg (it was previously outside) forwards sideways, diagonally across the arena. The horse should stay parallel to the sides of the arena; the hindquarters may not step into the arena more than the forehand. On the level of HB the horse is about five metres away from the track, the horse is straightened for one horse's length, then changed slightly onto the other bend and in the same way is ridden back to the track.

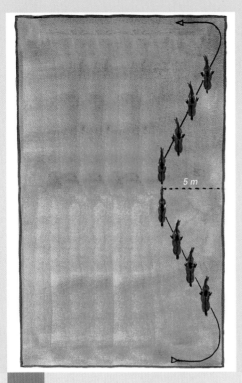

5 m

Groundpoles and cavaletti

Providing entertainment keeps the young horse interested. The simplest way is by using three to five poles and later on cavaletti (maximum height 30cm). Riding over poles improves the muscles, centre of gravity, ability and dexterity of the horse, giving the rider more control. It is also excellent preparation for jumping!

Distances between poles or cavaletti in the walk are about 80 centimetres, for trot 1.30 metres and canter 3.00 metres. The rider controls the horse with the legs to inhibit any running out and follows any stretch of the neck with soft hands, riding in the jumping seat.

The horse is only slightly bent and steps forwards twice as much as sideways.

Riding over cavaletti. The horse moves with lowered nose and rounded back.

When going up, the horse should lengthen and push from behind. Going downhill the horse collects himself to carry weight on the hindquarters.

Hacking in the countryside

Riding in the country is an absolute necessity! It strengthens the psyche of the horse and promotes the trust between horse and rider. The unevenness of the terrain and riding up and down hills are fabulous exercise, and improve the obedience of the horse as an added bonus. Objects such as tractors, cows, sheep, machinery or even plastic bags can be scary for a young horse, however, so beware.

Staying calm and keeping the aids clear are the only way forward, as spurs and crop often increase fear. Out in the country the rider can practise everything learnt in the arena: half-halts, correct bend around a corner, even some lengthening of stride if the path allows for that. Going uphill enables the horse to push from behind, while riding downhill permits collecting the horse to some extent to take the weight onto the hindquarters.

A harmonious ride on a well-schooled horse is the reward for consistent work. Trouble and sweat forgotten – only happiness remains. Photo: C. Slawik

Comment

All dressage work is essentially no more than a means to an end. The purpose of working in an arena is to achieve the following goals:

- The horse will be a pleasure to ride, obedient, soft and energetic.
- The horse will become more beautiful, developing muscles in the right places and becoming content.

- The horse will live longer! Learning to carry more weight behind relieves the forelegs; heart and lungs are trained and kept fit.

However, too much specialised training at a very young age can be detrimental to the horse, just as starting to ride too early is! A solid basic training is as important for the young horse as it is for the young rider.

Imprint

Copyright of original edition © 2001 by Cadmos Verlag
This edition © 2002 by Cadmos Equestrian
Translation: Desiree Gerber
Design and composition: Ravenstein Brain Pool
Photographs: P. Prohn, C.Slawik
Drawings: Esther von Hacht
Printed by Westermann Druck, Zwickau
All rights reserved.
Copying or storage in electronic media is permitted only
with the prior written permission of the publisher.
Printed in Germany.
ISBN 3-86127-932-0

OTHER CADMOS BOOKS

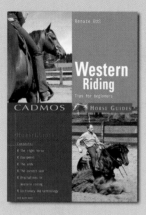

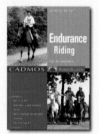
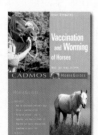
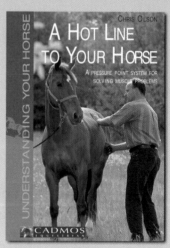